Computer Hacking

Learn computer hacking for beginners on everything from how to hack, powerful hacking techniques, underground methods, hacking skills, and much more.

Table Of Contents

Introduction

I want to thank you and congratulate you for downloading the book "Computer Hacking".

This book contains proven steps and strategies on how to become a truly good at hacking websites.

Here's an inescapable fact: you will need to practice your skills in order to hone them in and become a hacking master.

If you do not develop your own technique right away, do not fret, it will become easier and easier every time you practice.

It's time for you to become an amazing hacker by diving into the information that is provided in this book.

Chapter 1: Definition of a Hacker

There is a shared culture or community of programmers, as well as networking wizards that is traced through history for decades from the first sharing minicomputers and the earliest experiments with ARPAnet. This community ended up with the term hacker. Hackers have built the Internet. Unix is made from the techniques, skills, and languages that the hackers perfected. If you have actually contributed to the Internet and others know you as a hacker, then you are a hacker.

There is a mindset that comes along with being a hacker. It is not just confined to the stereotypical software type hacker. There are many who have applied the hacker attitude to many things like music or electronics. You can find it in the highest levels of any art or science. However, this book is concentrated on the software type of hacker, as well as the culture that comes with it.

It is extremely important to know the difference between a hacker and a cracker. Most people think they are one in the same. You will run across many people who claim to be a hacker, but they are really crackers. How do you know the difference? To put it quite simply, a hacker creates things, whereas a cracker breaks them. For example, have you ever tried to get into someone else's email or social media account? This is not hacking. This is cracking. You are "breaking" into something. In all actuality, crackers anger hackers as they give the hackers a bad name. Hackers pride themselves in creating code to manipulate technology; they don't break it to gain something. Hackers view crackers as irresponsible and lazy. Breaking security does not make you a hacker, just like hot-wiring a sports car does not make you a mechanic. If you want to become a hacker, then go ahead and read on. If you want to a cracker, read a different book.

Ultimately, hackers believe that information should be free, built upon, and shared. For example, you can read many retrieved documents or information that has been gathered from hackers and leaked out to the public by visiting the Wikileaks official site. (wikileaks.org)

***Important Note: Hacking is illegal in most forms. If you are learning on how to hack for testing security, move on. Everything within this book is to be performed at your own risk and the author is not held responsible for any legal action taken.**

Chapter 2: Attitude of a Hacker

Hackers actually solve problems and help create things. They believe in voluntary and freedom of help. In order to be accepted, you will have to behave as if you have this attitude. If you think of having the attitude just to be accepted into this culture, then you are definitely missing the point. Hacking is almost a way of life, as well as dominating the Internet and technology. Adapting this attitude is important for you, to help you learn, as well as to keep you motivated in your venture. As with all of the arts, the most successful way to become a hacker is to emulate the mindsets of the master hackers, not just their intellect, but emotionally as well. Read this Zen poem, you will get it.

To follow the path;

Look to the master.

Follow the master;

Walk with the master.

See through the master;

Become the master.

Here are the ways to help bring on the mindset of a hacker. Follow the steps and practice them until they become second nature.

1.There are fascinating problems everywhere, just waiting to be solved.

Being a hacker can be a lot of fun, but it is a type of fun that will take some work. It takes motivation. Professional athletes do not just become amazing overnight or just because they choose too. They have to work at it; just like the master hackers. You have to push yourself. In order to become a hacker you will have a thrill when it comes to problem solving. You will enjoy sharpening the skill set, and you will love to exercise your own intelligence. If you are not like this naturally, you will need to become one. You need to have faith in your capabilities of learning. Remember to tackle one piece of the problem at a time. You will learn as you do.

2. Never solve a problem twice.

Creative people are priceless, and very limited. Those creative people should not waste their time on re-inventing an invention. There are other problems just waiting to be solved. You should never set out to re-invent the wheel. In order to behave like the hacker, you must believe that time is precious; so much so that it is almost like a moral duty; to share information, give solutions, and solve the problems that are identified. Often times, there are many things that are learned from each problem. It is all right and sometimes necessary to decide what could be done better through the solving of a problem. What is not all right is legal, artificial, or institutional barriers that will stop a good solution from being used or reused and then force people to re-invent the wheels. For example, using closed source code.

3. Drudgery and boredom is completely evil.

Creative people, hackers included, should never have to drudge through repetitive work or become bored. When this happens it means that they are not doing what it is they do best. This waste of time hurts everyone.

4. Freedom is best.

Hackers are normally anti-authoritarians. Anyone who is able to give orders that can stop a hacker from solving a problem falls into this group and is viewed as unintelligent by the hacker. The authoritarians thrive on secrecy and censorship, and they distrust cooperation or information sharing; they love being in control. Therefore, in order to behave like the hacker, you will need to develop an instinctive type of hostility towards censorship, the use of force, the use of deception to compel adults, and secrecy. You will need to be willing to act on the belief.

5. Attitude isn't a substitute for competence.

In order to become a hacker, you will need to develop some of these types of attitudes. However, copping the attitude will not make you a hacker. Becoming the hacker will take practice, intelligence, hard work, and dedication. Therefore, you need to learn to distrust attitude, as well as respect competence of any kind. Hacker will never allow posers to waste time, however, they will honor competences; especially when it comes to hacking. Competence at skills that very few can master is honored and competence at skills that involve the acuteness of mental capacity, concentration, and craft are even better. If you honor competence, you will enjoy developing it yourself. The hard work, as well as the dedication will become a type of play that is intense and will not feel like work at all.

Chapter 3: Basic Hacking Skills

The attitude of a hacker is crucial; however, the skills are even more crucial. Attitude is not a substitute for competence. There is a specific toolkit of skills that you will need to have before becoming a hacker. The toolkit will change slowly over the course of time as technology offers the creation of new skills and makes some of the old ones obsolete. For example, you would have had to learn machine language since HTML was not created yet.

1. Learn how to program.

This is number one because it is detrimental to becoming a hacker. If you do not know any of the computer languages, it is recommended to start with the Python language. It is designed very clean; very well documented, and is relatively kind to the beginners. Despite being a good language to learn first, it isn't a toy. This language is extremely powerful, as well as flexible. It is great for large projects. There are many great tutorials that will walk you through learning Python. If a language offers you a large amount of tasks that you can perform with it, it is great to work on projects, but will not be great to learn hacking with.

If you decide to go serious with the programming, then you should learn C. It is the core language of Unix. C++ is extremely close to C. Learning one of these will be pretty simple once you start. C is extremely efficient and extremely sparing of the machine's resources like memory. All the low level code is complex and will soak up a large amount of the time on debugging. With the machines of today, this isn't a problem due to the power they offer.

LISP is definitely worth learning for another reason. The insightful clarification experience that you will have once you finally get it is priceless. This program will enhance or provide you with amazing programming skills. Here are five of the languages that would be good for you to learn:

1. C
2. C++
3. Java
4. LISP
5. Perl

2. Get an open-source Unix and then learn to use it.

Having a computer should be appreciated and understand the magnitude of what it really means. Hacker culture was originated back when the computers were really expensive that most people could not have one. The single most crucial step for any newbie is to get a copy of one of the BSD-Unixes or Linux. Install it on your computer and learn to run it. There are other operating systems; however, the other operating systems are distributed in binary. You cannot read their codes and you cannot modify it. Learning how to hack using a Microsoft Windows machine or with another closed source system is like trying to dance while wearing a full body cast.

Using a Mac OS X is possible; however, only part of this system is open source. You are likely to hit many walls and you will have to be very careful not to develop a habit of depending on the Apple's proprietary codes. If you concentrate on Unix, you can learn many useful things.

The operating system of the Internet is Unix. While you are able to learn how to use the Internet without knowing Unix, you cannot be a hacker of the Internet without knowing Unix. For tis reason alone, the hacker community is strongly centered on Unix. Learn and play around with Linux.

3. Learn how to write HTML.

Most of the aspects in hacker culture have been built to do work out of sight. It helps run factories and even offices. It helps run universities without obvious impact on how regular peoples live. The Web is a large exception; the large shiny toy that even the politicians admit has changed our way of life. Because of this, you will need to learn how to work it. This does not mean that you need to just learn how to drive the browser, but you will need to learn how to write HTML, which is the language of the Web. If you do not know how to program, then writing HTML will help teach you some of the mental habits that will aid in the learning of programing. Trying building a home page using only HTML. Make it to help hackers and ensure that it has good content.

4. If English is not your first language, become fluent.

There are many hackers all over the globe, but any hacker will tell you that English is the working language of the culture, as well as the Internet. You will need to know English in order to function in the community. For example, even if there are two hackers of the same native tongue, they tend to speak English. Keeping this in mind, hackers will ignore you if you do not write grammatically correct or your writing is riddled with a lot of misspellings and other mistakes. When you seek help with different things, then you will be ignored if you do not follow English basics.

Chapter 4: Learning HTML

In this chapter you are going to learn the basics of HTML. Just like everything that is learned, practice makes perfect. You will also be given project ideas in order to help you hone in on the HTML skills you are about to pick up.

Definition of HTML

HTML is actually a markup language that is used for describing web documents like web pages. HTML stands for the term Hyper Text Markeup Language. Markup language is a set of markup tags, which are described as HTML tags (HTML documents). Each of the HTL tags describes different content of the document.

Example of HTML:

<!DOCTYPE html?

<html>

<head>

<title>Page Title</title>

</head>

<body>

```
<h1>Your First Heading</h1>

<p>This is the first paragraph in your
content.</p>

</body>

</html>
```

Explanation of Example:

- **DOCTYPE** is the declaration that defines this
  document as **HTML**.
- The text in between **<html>** and the **</html>**
  describes the document.
- The text between the **<head>** and the **</head>**
  offers the information about this document.
- The text in between **<title>** and the **</title>**
  offers a title for this document.
- The text between the **<body>** and the
  </body> describes the content.
- The text between the **<h1>** and the **</h1>**
  describes the heading in the document.
- The text between the **<p>** and the **</p>** offers
  the description of the paragraphs in the
  content.

HTML Tags

The tags of HTML are keywords that are surrounded
by the angle brackets. In order to see a full example
of HTML coding, visit your favorite website. Right
click on the background, and then click "inspect

element". You will be able to see the coding that is used for this website.

EXAMPLE: <tagname>your content</tagname>

- The tags will come in pairs like <body> and </body>.
- The first of the tags in the pair is called the start tag or opening tag. The second tag is called the end tag or closing tag.
- The end tag will always be written like the start tag, but will have a slash before the tag name.

Internet Browsers

The main purpose of a browser like Chrome, Firefox, IE, and Safari is to be able to read HTML documents and display them for you. The browser does not display the tags; however, they use them to determine how the document should be displayed.

Structure of HTML Pages

This is the way an HTML page should be structured when writing with HTML coding.

```
<html>

    <head>

        <title>Your Page Title</title>

    </head>
```

```
<body>

    <h1>This is Your Heading</h1>

    <p>This is a paragraph.</p>

    <p>This is another one of your paragraphs.</p>

    </body>

</html>
```

NOTE: Only the tag \<body\> will display on the browser.

\<!DOCTYPE\> Declaration

The \<!DOCTYPE\> declaration will help the browser display the web page in the correct manner. There are different types of documents on the web. In order to display the document in the correct manner, the browser has to know the type and the version. It is not case sensitive; all of the cases are perfectly acceptable.

- \<!DOCTYPE html\>
- \<!DOCTYPE HTML\>
- \<!doctype html\>
- \<!Doctype Html\>

Common Declaration

- **HTML5** - <!DOCTYPE html>
- **HTML 4.01** - <!DOCTYPE HTML PUBLIC "-//W3C//DTD HTML 4.01 Transitional//EN" http://www.w3.org/TR/html4/loose.dtd>
- **XHTML 1.0** - <!DOCTYPE html Public "-//W3C//DTD XHTML 1.0 Transitional//EN" http://www.w3.org/TR/xhtml1/STSxhtml1-transitional.dtd>

Versions of HTML

- HTML – 1991
- HTML 2.0 – 1995
- HTML 3.2 – 1997
- HTML 4.01 – 1999
- XHTML – 2000
- HTML5 – 2014

Editors for HTML

You can use different editors like:

- Microsoft Expression Web
- Adobe Dreamweaver
- CoffeeCup HTML Editor

However, when you are learning HTML it is recommended to use a text editor like Notepad or TextEdit. Notepad is on Windows and TextEdit is on Mac computers.

Steps for Creating Your First Page with TextEdit or Notepad.

We are going to assume that you are using Notepad for arguments sake.

Step 1: Notepad

Open up your Notepad.

Step 2: Write HTML

You will need to write or copy some of the HTML as follows:

<!DOCTYPE html>

<html>

<body>

<h1>Enter The First Heading</h1>

<p>Type your first paragraph.</p>

</body>

</html>

Step 3: Save Your Page

Save the file on the computer. Select 'File', then 'Save As' in the menu. Name your file "index.htm" or another name that will end with 'htm'.

Step 4: View the HTML Page

In order to view the page you just built, you will need to open your browser that you use to surf the net. In order to do this, find the file in the folder that it is housed in. Right click on it and click 'open with', then choose your browser.

HTML Headings

When you use headings you will have different tags. They begin at 1 (being the largest) up to 6 (being the smallest). Make sure to close the code line with the slash mark after the heading and leave no spaces other than the ones in the heading itself.

HTML Links

In order to create a link, there is a specific tag to use. The tag is "a". You will use it like this: <a href=http://sweetfreakings.com>Sweet Freakings Radio</a> The "href" is an attribute. Attributes are offered to provide additional information on the HTML elements.

HTML Images

The images are defined by the tag <img> tag. The source is "src". The alternative text is labeled with "alt". The size is specified by "width" and "height". Here is a sample code line for an image:

<img src=http://sweetfreakings.com/wp-content/uploads/2015/05/cropped-cropped-sfszombiecorn-middle23.png height="250" width="750" alt="Sweet Freakings">

Nested Elements

The elements of your page are "nested" inside the document. Here is an example of four different elements inside this sample text.

<!DOCTYPE html>

<html>

<body>

<h1>Enter The First Heading</h1>

<p>Type your first paragraph.</p>

</body>

</html>

Empty Elements

There are elements that have no content. They are called empty elements. The tag <br> offers a line with no content, but this is an example of a tag that has no ending tag. They are closed in the beginning like: </br>

Lang Attribute

The Lang Attribute is the attribute that you use to specify the language the page should be displayed in. The code will look like this:

<!DOCTYPE html>

<html lang="en-US">

<body>

<h1>Enter The First Heading</h1>

<p>Type your first paragraph.</p>

</body>

</html>

HTML Attributes

Here is a list of attributes that is used in HTML coding:

- alt- This specifies an alternative text for the image instead of the file name.

- disabled – This specifies an input element that should be disabled.
- id – This specifies an id for a certain element.
- Href – This specifies a URL for the link in the content.
- Src – This attribute specifies a source for a certain image.
- Style – This attribute specifies an inline CSS for an element.
- Title – This is additional information about a specific element.
- Value – This attribute is used to specify the value for the input element.

Chapter 5: Hack a Website

Here is a eight step process of hacking a website. Remember that hacking is illegal unless you are authorized or asked to do so by the site owner to access security. Just like using Google to do a search, you can use Google to find hacking tools. However, you will find a list of hacking tool within this book. Now that you have a basic understanding of how HTML works, you are on your way to hacking a site. This is just a beginner's activity, and sites that have maximum security is not able to be hacked in this manner.

Step 1: Open up the site you want to hack.

You will enter the wrong username and password to the site. Enter anything in those fields it does not matter. An error will happen and tell you that the information that you gave is incorrect. This is where the hacking will begin.

Step 2: View the source.

Right click anywhere on the page, and then click on "view source".

Step 3: Look at the source code.

You will see the HTML that was used for this page. You will look for code that looks similar to: <_form action="...Login..."> Right before this login information, copy the URL of the specific site, in which is: "<_form.....action=http://www.yourtargesite.com/login......>

Step 4: Delete the script from the above that validates the information in the server.

You will need to take extra care when you do this. The success of the hacking will depend on how efficient you are when deleting the script code that validates the account information.

Step 5: Look close for specific tags.

You will need to find <_input name-"password type="password"> and then replace it with <_type=password> with <_type=text>.

Step 6: Save the as a file.

You will need to save the page as a file, ensuring that the file has the ending ".html". Example: filename.html

Step 7: Open the web site.

Open up the site you saved to your hard disk. You will notice slight changes in the page this is supposed to happen.

Step 8: Provide a username.

You can enter any username and password. You will have successfully gained access to the site and the database information.

Chapter 6: Popular Hackers and Hacker Collectives

Here is a list of popular hackers or hacker collectives that have brought on a name for themselves. Some have landed in prison, while others are still hacking away. It is important to know that certain types of hacking are illegal.

Jonathan James

Jonathan was known as "comrade". He was convicted, and then sent to prison due to his hacking in the U.S. while he was still a minor. When he was only fifteen years old, he hacked into many networks that included those that belonged to Miami-Dade, Bell South, as well as NASA and the U.S. Department of Defense. Jonathan hacked into the NASA network and downloaded so much source code that he learned how the International Space Station actually worked. The value of the downloaded had the value of 1.7 million dollars. To add in more cost, NASA was forced to close the network for three weeks in order to investigate the breach, which cost another $41,000. In the year 2007, there were many high profile companies that were victim to a wave of malicious attacks. Even though Jonathan denied it, he was suspected, and then investigated. In the year 2008 he committed suicide because he thought he would be convicted of the crimes he didn't commit.

Kevin Mitnick

The story of Kevin Mitnick is so much cooler than Jonathan's sad story. Mitnick actually had movies made about him. He was classified as the "most wanted computer criminal in U.S. history." After serving an entire year in prison for hacking into the network of Digital Equipment Corporation, he was given a three year supervised release. Towards the end of the three year period, he fled an went on a hacking spree that lasted 2.5 years. It involved hacking into the national defense warning system, as well as stealing corporate secrets. He was eventually caught, and then convicted. He received a five year sentence. After he served his time, he became a consultant, as well as a public speaker about computer security. He is now running the Mitnick Security Consulting LLC.

Kevin Poulsen

Kevin was known as "Dark Dante" and was able to use his talents to rig a radio station's phone line to always be the winning caller. He actually won a Porsche. Media had called him the "Hannibal Lecter of computer crime." He then was put on the FBI's wanted list after he hacked the system and stole some wiretap information. He was caught in a grocery store, and then sentences to 51 months in prison, as well as a fine for restitution of $56,000. Much like Mitnick, Kevin changed his ways once released.

He even helped law enforcement catch 744 sex offenders that were on MySpace. He is now a journalist and senior editor for Wired News.

Gary McKinnon

Gary McKinnon was known as "Solo". He coordinated the largest military hacks of all time. The allegations are that Gary, over a 13 month time period in 2001 to March 2002, he illegally gained access to 97 different computers that belonged to the United States Armed Forces, as well as NASA. Gary claimed that he was only looking for information that was related to UFO cover-ups and free energy suppression. However, according to the United States authorities, he deleted many critical files, which rendered over 300 computers unusable and resulted in over $700,000 in government damages. Since Gary was Scottish and did this out of the United Kingdom, he was able to escape the government for a bit. As of today, he is still fighting to stop being expedited to the United States.

Anonymous

Anonymous is by far one of the most notorious and publicized groups. They are an underground, international network of 'hacktivists' that have sprung up from 4Chan, a controversial image based bulleting board. This collective has been put in the public's eye since the year 2008 when it was originally shared on YouTube. In this video, the tagline for this collective was publicized.

"Knowledge is free. We are Anonymous. We are Legion. We do not forgive. We do not forget. Expect us."

Since the public knowledge of the existence of this collective, they have launched attacks on different governmental department websites, multi-nationals, politicians, hundreds of ISIS

Twitter accounts, the Church of Scientology, and more. It is important to understand that due to Anonymous being decentralized, there is no specific leadership spearheading any campaigns. Most of the attacks consist of different individuals who are working toward the same goal.

One of the goals that they came together on was to launch an attack against VISA, Mastercard, and PayPal in response of the leash that they had around Wikileaks. Wikileaks is dependent on donations in order to maintain operation. The United States government mobilized a plane to make the donations impossible. This in turn would strangle the website and kill it. Anonymous did not like tis and they moved in with Operation Avenge Assange. They used a LOIC (low orbit ion cannon) tool. This tool allowed anyone to a DDOS (denial of service) attack on these high profile websites. It took them to their knees and lost millions of dollars during the process. They attacked Mexican drug cartels, child pornography websites, and even the Israeli Government, and it doesn't stop there.

Syrian Electronic Army

Syrian Electronic Army is also referred to as SEA. They have been acting in support of President Bashar al Assad. Therefore, SEA is typically attacking the Western media outlets that publish any negative press on him. The university students behind the attacks have gained much respect from the online security firms after hacking into hundreds of sites. Some targets include CBC, the New York Times, and the Washington Post. This caused many to become concerned about the motives of the group.

Chapter 7: Hacker Tools

Here is a list of tools that you can use to hack, along with their description.

nmap

This is an open source hacker tool. The name stands for "Network Mapper." It is used to discover networks, as well as security auditing. There are many different system admins that use nmap to aid in network inventory, managing service upgrade schedules, open ports, and monitoring the host or service uptime. This tool uses a raw IP packet in creative ways in order to determine what hosts are available on a network, what services those hosts offer, what the operating systems are, and what type and version of a packet filter or firewall is being used.

Metasploit

This is a largely popular pen testing or hacking tool that can be used by cyber security professionals or even ethical hackers. Metasploit is a computer security project that offers information about security vulnerabilities and will help to formulate the penetration testing and the IDS testing.

Burp Suite

Burp Suite includes many different features that will aid in the penetration tester or the ethical hacker. There are two commonly used applications within the tool that includes the Burp Suite Spider. It can enumerate and then map out different pages and the parameters of the site by examining cookies. It will then initiate the connections between these applications.

Angry IP Scanner

Angry IP Scanner is also called IP scan. It is a freely available, open source and cross platform hacking scanner that is both easy and fast to use. The main purpose of this tool is to scan IP addresses and the ports to find open ports and doors.

Cain & Abel

Cain & Abel is a tool to recover passwords and is mainly used for Microsoft OS. This is a popular hacking tool that will allow a user to seek a recovery of a wide range of passwords by sniffing a network, and cracking the encrypted passwords using a dictionary. Cain, can also record VoIP conversation, decode different hashed scrambled passwords, recover the wireless network keys, and so much more. If you need a password-cracking platform, then you can use this.

Ettercap

Ettercap is very popular and is used by many cyber security professionals. It works by putting the users network interface into a promiscuous mode and by poisoning the target machines. Once it is successful, Ettercap is able to deploy different attack on their victims. It can also support many different plugins.

Conclusion

Thank you again for downloading this book!

I hope this book was able to help you to help you better understand how to become a hacker and what it takes to be great.

The next step is to pick the language you would like to begin with and get to practicing.

Finally, if you enjoyed this book, please take the time to share your thoughts and post a review on Amazon. It'd be greatly appreciated!

Thank you and good luck!

Description:

From HTML to amazing hacking tools, you will be able to dive into the culture that is hacking. Hacking attitude, mindset, and even how to break into a website is included for security purposes. Included is a list of programming languages to begin with and many other tips. In this book you will also learn about high profile hackers and collectives from their beginning to where they are now. If you ever dreamed of being a hacker, you need to start with this book.

www.ingramcontent.com/pod-product-compliance
Lightning Source LLC
Chambersburg PA
CBHW060934050326
40689CB00013B/3081